COMPUTING FOR BEGINNERS

WINDOWS 8.1 EXPLAINED IN PLAIN ENGLISH

Lynn Stephen

CONTENTS

INTRODUCTION

This book covers the new updated version of Windows 8.1. Windows 8.1 is primarily for touch screen devices, i.e. smart phones, tablets and touch screen computers. However this book covers Windows 8.1 on a desktop computer or laptop.

I have written in an easy to understand manner in plain English cutting out all the computer jargon which seems to confuse so many people. The opening chapters will cover the basics of your computer i.e. your computer, monitor, keyboard and mouse and these chapters are for those of you who are completely new to computers.

The following chapters cover Broadband, the importance of Anti-Virus Software, Getting Started with Windows 8.1, Using the Internet, Email, Adding Contacts, Photos and backing up your work. There is also a chapter covering files and folders.

I hope you will find this book useful and that it will help you find your way around your new computer.

CHAPTER ONE

YOUR COMPUTER

When you buy a new computer it will usually consist of four main components, the computer, the monitor (screen), the keyboard and the mouse. If you opt for a laptop, all the components are together. You may also have a printer.

Before I go into detail regarding these items, I would like to explain a few words you may across which may cause some confusion regarding your computer:

a. **HARDWARE** - the main components of your computer (tower, monitor, keyboard, mouse, and printer) are known as hardware. Hardware refers to components which you can see. All of these components work together and are connected via cables to your computer tower.

b. **SOFTWARE** - to enable a computer to function it must use software. Software is a program which is either pre-installed onto your computer or which comes on a CD/DVD. The CD or DVD would be inserted into the CD drive on your computer which would enable the relevant program to be installed onto your computer. Once the software has been installed it will stay on your computer's hard drive. The CD will be removed and kept in a safe place. A good example of software is your word processing program, Microsoft Word.

c. **OPERATING SYSTEM** - Windows 8.1 is your operating system. This is the most important piece of software on your computer. Without it your computer will not work. It is called "Windows" because every time you open a new file or program, it will open in a new window. The window can be made to fill the whole screen or can be minimized or restored down to one third of its size.

d. **HARD DRIVE** (C: Drive) - this is the main storage in your computer and is located inside your tower or laptop so it is not actually visible.

e. **CD/DVD DRIVE** - this refers to a drawer on the front of your computer or on the side of your laptop, into which you insert CDs or DVDs to either install a program or to listen to music or watch a film.

Types of Computer

Two examples of a computer.
Tower and Shuttle computer.

Although people still call their computer a tower, nowadays computers are much smaller and can sit on your desk.

A lot of people believe it is the monitor which is the computer, which is an easy mistake to make, as it is the monitor you are looking at when you are using the computer.

It is on the front of the computer that the power button is located. This is the button which will turn your computer on (known as booting up). There may also be a smaller button on the front of the computer which is the reset button. This will enable you to restart your computer without completely turning it off (known as rebooting). You may need to use this button should everything on your computer freeze but don't worry too much as this doesn't happen much these days.

Also on the front of your computer there will be a disc drawer with a small button next to it which, when pressed will open the drawer and it is here that you will place a CD or DVD.

CHAPTER TWO

THE MONITOR

The monitor or screen is where you will see all the images on your computer and all the text which you type in. When you first switch on your computer you will see a small arrow in the centre of the screen, this is called the cursor. The cursor is positioned on objects on the screen using your mouse. You will then click on the object and the program will open.

CHAPTER THREE

THE KEYBOARD

The keyboard is used to type text which will appear on the screen. The main keys on a keyboard are arranged in the same way as on a typewriter. There are two main types of keyboard, a wired keyboard i.e. one which is connected to your computer via a cable and the other is a wireless keyboard which has a USB dongle which is plugged into your computer. The wireless keyboard will pick up the signal from the dongle in your computer. This will then enable you to use your keyboard without being restricted by a wire.

I will now explain the keys on your keyboard. There are many different types of keyboard which may be laid out in different ways with shortcut keys but generally the main keys are the same.

ESC key. This is the escape key and can be used in various situations. Some programs will tell you to press the escape key to get out of the program. People who play games on their computers often use this key to exit the game. Another example of its use is on the Internet when you have a program such as BBC iplayer playing on full screen, you

7

would need to press this key to return to a normal size screen.

F KEYS. Along the top of your keyboard you will see a row of keys from F1 to F12. These keys are called Function keys and generally they are not used when you are beginning. The exception being the F1 key which will bring up a help menu in any program and the F4 key which, when pressed with the Alt key, will close the current window. As a beginner, you can ignore these keys.

PRINT SCREEN, SCROLL LOCK AND PAUSE BREAK KEYS. These are located next to the function keys. The Print Screen key enables you to take a screenshot of the image you are viewing and save it or send it by email. The Scroll Lock key is used mainly in Excel which is a spreadsheet program and it enables you to move the window without moving the selected cell. The Pause Break key, when pressed with the Windows logo key, will bring up information about your computer.

TAB key. On many word processing programs, there are pre-set tabs on the page and each time you press the tab key you will move to the next tab point on the page. You can also set your own tabs on a page. When filling out forms on the Internet i.e. when registering on a website, you are asked to fill in several boxes; name, address, email address etc. By pressing the tab key you can quickly move to the next box without having to use your mouse.

CAPS LOCK key. When this key is pressed once, everything you type will be in capital letters. Remember to press it again to return to normal typing.

SHIFT key. The shift key is used to type one capital letter. Hold this key down while you press the required letter. As soon as it is released you will return to normal type. You have two Shift keys, one at each end of the keyboard. You will notice on your keyboard several keys with multiple characters. By holding down the shift key and pressing the relevant key you will type the character at the top of this key (by pressing number 1 you will type the exclamation mark which is at the top of this key).

CTRL key. This is the Control key which when pressed with other keys will enable you to take various shortcuts depending on which program you are in at the time. Pressing CTRL and S will save your work, CTRL and P will print your work.

WINDOWS LOGO key. This key when pressed will bring up the start screen. Also when you are in a program, pressing this key will return you to the start screen. In Windows 8.1 you will probably use this key at lot.

ALT key. This key is used for various shortcuts. i.e. Alt and F4 will close the window currently open.

THE SPACEBAR. This is the long key at the bottom of your keyboard and is used to put a space between words.

THE FOUR DIRECTIONAL ARROW KEYS. The up and down arrows will enable you to scroll the page up and down. When in a word processing program all four directional arrows can be used to move around the page. The left and right keys can be used on your Start Screen to enable you to view all tiles.

ENTER key. This key is used to give a command to your computer. If you are searching for something on the Internet, after you have typed a subject into the search box, by pressing the Enter key this will send the information and give you the results. In a word processing program, pressing the enter key will take you to the next line.

BACKSPACE and DELETE keys. These keys are used to delete typed text. By pressing the backspace key once, you will delete the last letter typed to the left of the cursor. By pressing the delete key once, you will delete the last letter typed to the right of the cursor. If you hold either of these keys down it will continue to delete until the relevant key is released. The backspace key can also be used on the Internet to go back to the previous page.

INSERT key. This key is used in word processing to overtype everything to the right of the cursor. Simply press the Insert key and whatever you type will replace the words already there. Don't forget to press it again to revert to normal typing.

HOME and END keys. These keys can be used in conjunction with the CTRL key. For example if you press CTRL and Home you will immediately be taken to the top of the page. Similarly if you press CTRL and End you will be taken to the bottom of the page.

PAGE UP and PAGE DOWN keys. These keys do exactly as they say. By pressing page up the page will move up and by pressing page down, the page will move down.

NUM LOCK key. This key has two uses. If you press this key so the function is on, you can type the numbers from the small panel on the right of the keyboard. If you press it again and take the function off, the keys on this small panel can be used to scroll around your page.

NUM LOCK, CAP LOCK, SCROLL LOCK indicator lights on the keyboard inform you if any of these functions are on. If the light is on, the function is on. For example if the Cap Lock light is on, this is an indicator that you have chosen to type in capital letters.   I find this is a very useful reminder as it is very easy to forget to turn the cap lock off.

CTRL, ALT and DELETE. By holding these keys down all at the same time, you can end a non-responsive program. Pressing the keys will take you to a screen where you can click on task manager where you will then see all running programs. Just click on the non-responsive program in the list, then click on "end task" at the bottom.

CHAPTER FOUR

THE MOUSE

The mouse is a device which you use to point to things on the screen. When you move the mouse you will see a small arrow (cursor) on the computer screen. You use the cursor to select the desired program or object. The cursor must be on the program or object concerned. You will then be required to click, either once or twice, on the program to open it.

There are two types of mice; a wired mouse which is connected to your computer via a cable or a wireless mouse which has a USB dongle which is connected to your computer. The wireless mouse then picks up the signal from the dongle in your computer and you are not restricted by a wire.

The mouse has several different functions. Before we can begin you need to know how to use your mouse.

It is a good idea to place your hand over the mouse so you feel comfortable and relaxed and so that your index finger on your right hand (assuming you are right handed) is resting over the left hand button of the mouse. Ideally with your hand relaxed you can now move your mouse to position the cursor on the required program or object and then click on the object without taking your eyes off the screen.

Don't worry if you are having difficulty in controlling your mouse, everyone has trouble at first - just try and relax your hand.

Mouse Functions

Left Click - this means you should use the left side of your mouse to click once on the specified object or program. This is the most frequently used function of the mouse and is used to give the computer an instruction. Although a double left click is often used to get into a program, it is nearly always a single left click when you are in the actual program.

Double Click - this instruction is used to open a program, folder, file etc. You should click on the left side of the mouse twice in quick succession.

Right click - by clicking on an object using the right side of the mouse, you will be presented with a menu specific to the item you have just clicked on.

Scroll - almost every mouse will have a scroll wheel in the centre. You can move this wheel forward and back which in turn will move your page up and down. Just gently roll the wheel either up and down. Don't press too hard on this scroll wheel otherwise the page will scroll out of control. If this does happen, press the wheel again and it should return to normal.

Drag - this involves placing your cursor on an item, holding down the left side of the mouse and keeping it held down, dragging the item to the desired position. This function can be used on the Start screen to rearrange the tiles displayed here. This is also useful when placing files into folders.

CHAPTER FIVE

PRINTERS

There are many different Printers and it would be impossible for me to go into detail on any of these as the printer you buy would probably be different.

However most people nowadays will opt for an "All in One Printer". This is a printer, scanner and photo-copier all in one machine. These are very popular and very useful.

Most are stand-alone photo-copiers so you do not need to switch your computer on to take a photo-copy.

You can scan documents or photos from your all-in-one printer to your computer and view them on the screen.

If you are using a laptop then it is a good idea to buy a wireless printer, in which case the printer could be in one room and you can print from another room. This is ideal if you do not have much room.

You can also use a wireless printer with a desktop computer but if you have room and can place the printer near your computer then I think to have it connected by a wire is a better way to go.

CHAPTER SIX

LAPTOPS

If you have chosen a laptop then everything already written is relevant to you but I will cover the basic differences between a laptop and a desktop computer.

With a laptop, instead of having four different components to make your computer work, everything is contained within one machine.

When you open your laptop you will see the keyboard at the bottom and the screen at the top. The power button on your laptop will be positioned somewhere just above the keys on the keyboard. Press this once and your laptop will power on.

On the keyboard just below the spacebar, you will see a small rectangle pad. This is called your touchpad and it is this pad which you will use to control your cursor, in the same way you would use a  mouse on a desktop computer. You move your finger gently over this pad and you will see the cursor on the screen move. You can now position the cursor on an item. Just below the touchpad, there are two buttons and these correspond to the left and right buttons on a mouse. Pressing the left button corresponds to a left click on a mouse. On the touchpad, be careful not to go too close to the right and bottom sides of the pad when you are first starting out as these have scroll functions on. If you accidentally move your finger up and down on the right side, you will notice the page zoom up or down. Just move away from the right side of the touchpad and it will return to normal.

These scroll functions on the touchpad can be used to scroll the page up and down in addition to the up and down directional arrow keys on the keyboard.

If you have trouble mastering the touchpad, and many people do, you can always use a wireless mouse instead. You would plug in the USB dongle which comes with a wireless mouse into the relevant slot on your laptop and the mouse will pick up the signal. You can now use the mouse as you would with a desktop computer.

On the side of your laptop you will have a CD/DVD drive drawer and in the centre of this drawer you will see a small raised button. Press this once and the drawer will pop out. Place a CD/DVD in the drawer and push the drawer back in to play the disc.

Charging your Laptop

Your laptop will have come with a battery and a charger/power lead. It is important not to overcharge your laptop as this will dramatically reduce the life of your machine. Ideally you should plug your laptop in and use on mains power until the battery is fully charged. Once fully charged, you should unplug your laptop and use on battery power. Once the battery gets low, a message will appear on the screen asking you to switch to mains power. This is the time to again plug your laptop in. You can easily see the status of your battery by moving your cursor to the bottom right of the screen and positioning it over the battery symbol (no need to click). It will now show you the battery percentage and how much time you have left before you need to charge it again.

CHAPTER SEVEN

BROADBAND

Most people who buy a computer want it for searching the Internet and sending emails. To be able to do this you need to apply for broadband. This is usually provided by the company who supplies your phone line. After you have ordered broadband, you will be sent a hub/router by the phone company and you will be given an activation date when your broadband will go live, after which time you are ready to use the internet. Your hub must be connected to your computer to enable you to use the Internet. With your hub, you will be supplied with filters (usually two) and these are plugged into your phone socket, another lead (usually grey) is plugged into the filter and the other end is plugged into the hub. If you are connecting wirelessly, i.e. to a laptop, you may need someone with computer knowledge to assist you. If you are connecting to a desktop computer then you would plug the Ethernet cable (again this would have been supplied with the hub) into the back of your computer and the other end into the back of your hub. You are now ready to start using the Internet.

There are many broadband deals on the market at the moment and it may be wise to seek advice before ordering. Broadband is usually paid monthly by direct debit to the provider.

CHAPTER EIGHT

ANTI-VIRUS SOFTWARE

It is very important for you to have up-to-date anti-virus software installed on your computer to eliminate the possibility of your computer being infected with a virus. If you are unfortunate enough to be infected with a virus, your computer will become unresponsive and you will need to seek help from a computer engineer to remove the virus. This may involve you losing all your files and programs as your hard drive may have been infected and will need to be formatted and Windows reinstalled.

There are many expensive anti-virus programs on the market but these are really not necessary. Windows 8.1 comes with a free anti-virus program from Microsoft called Windows Defender. Most anti-virus programs will update themselves automatically.

Many people are under the impression that if they have an anti-virus program installed on their computer they are protected. This is not the case unless you regularly scan your computer for viruses. To do this you must first click on Windows Defender (if it is on your start screen) and the following screen will appear.

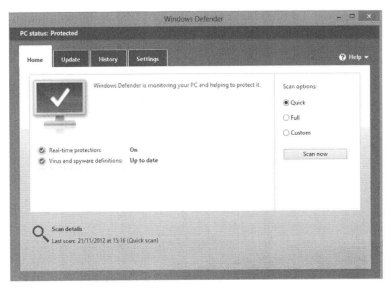

Click in the circle to the left of "full" and then click on "Scan Now". That is all you have to do.

You can then minimize the window by clicking on the _ at the top right of the window and you now get on with something else while the scan is taking place.

It is advisable to carry out regular scans of your computer and I would recommend doing a full scan once a month and a quick scan once a week.

Obviously you cannot be 100% sure you will never get a virus but having anti-virus software reduces this risk dramatically.

CHAPTER NINE

WINDOWS (resizing and scrolling)

Above is a picture of a window which I have opened in Microsoft Word which is a word processing program. Windows are the same whatever program you are in and the above is just an example.

Resizing Windows

On the top right hand corner of this window you will see three buttons.

By clicking once on - which in the minimize button, this will appear to close the window altogether but actually what you have done is put it on the taskbar below so it is still open but out of the way. To get the window back, just click once on the program displayed on the taskbar and it will be restored to full size.

By clicking on — which is the restore down/maximize — button, the window you are working on, which at the moment fills the whole screen and is full size, will resize itself down to about a third of its actual size. If you click this button again, you will restore the window back to its full size. Sometimes when you open a new window, it won't be full size so you will have to click on the maximize button to make it fill the screen.

The X is the button which will close the window altogether. This is the button you always press to exit the program you are working on.

If you are working in a word processing or similar program and haven't saved your work before clicking on the cross you will be asked if you want to save the changes you have made to your work. You should click on Yes if you wish to save the changes.

Scrolling with Windows

On the right hand side of every window is a scroll bar with small arrows at either end. By clicking on the bottom arrow this will scroll the page up and you will eventually reach the bottom of the page. Similarly by clicking on the top arrow you can scroll the page down until you reach the top. By using either of these arrows the page will move up or down one click at a time. You can also scroll the page up or down by placing your cursor over the bar between the two arrows and whilst holding down the left button on the mouse drag the page up and down.

Some windows also have a scroll bar at the bottom and again the same principal will apply. The left and right arrows will move the window to the left or right and again the bar can be moved in the same way as above.

You can also use the scroll wheel in the centre of your mouse to move the page up and down.

CHAPTER TEN

GETTING STARTED WITH WINDOWS 8.1

Start Screen Explained

It's now time to start using your computer. When you first switch on, you will see something very different from all the other Windows operating systems. Push the power button and a screen similar to the following will appear.

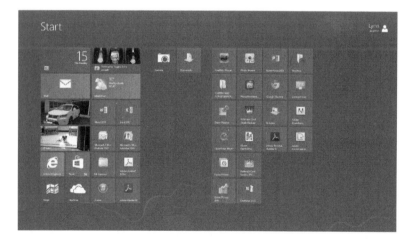

This screen is called the Start Screen. On the Start screen you will see various tiles which represent programs, apps or shortcuts to programs which are installed on your computer. This screen can be easily customized; you can change the background, move the tiles around or delete tiles you do not want. The tiles on the start screen should represent the programs or apps you will be using the most so any you do not require you can remove from this screen.

To move from one end of the Start Screen to the other, in order to view all tiles, press the Home or End keys on your keyboard. Alternatively you can use the directional buttons on your keyboard to move around the tiles. You can also just roll the wheel on your mouse and the page will move along.

Desktop Tile

You will see that one of the tiles on your start screen is called Desktop. For those of you who have changed from Windows XP, Vista or 7 to Windows 8.1, by clicking on this tile, you will be presented with a more familiar view of Windows.

How To open and close a Program

To go into a program from your start screen, you simply click once on the relevant tile and the program will open. When you wish to come out of this program, there are two ways in which you can do this. Firstly you can simply press the windows key on your keyboard or if you place your cursor at the top of the screen, the following bar will appear.

Just click on the cross which is on the right hand side and the program will be closed.

If the tile you have selected opens up in your desktop view then you will have the following three symbols at the top right of the page.

These represent (from left to right) minimize, maximize/restore down and close.

To come out of a program just click on the close symbol in the top right corner and the program will close. The minimize symbol will minimize the window (it will appear to have been closed but is actually on the taskbar at the bottom of the screen). By clicking on the maximize/restore down symbol this will make the window a third of its size and by clicking on it again it will take it back to full screen.

If you wish to access a program which you cannot see on your Start Screen, simply move your cursor on the screen and a small arrow will appear below your tiles. Click on this and the following screen will then appear.

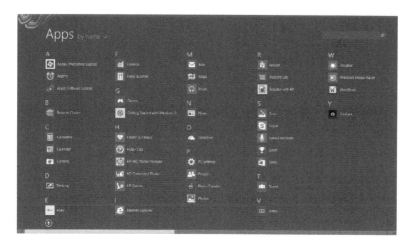

You can access a program from here by just clicking on it or if you want to move any of these programs to your Start Screen for easy access then all you do is right click on the

33

program required and you will see a small menu has appeared – see following picture.

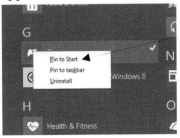

Click on "Pin to Start" and this program tile will now be on your Start Screen. If you click on pin to taskbar then the program will be pinned to the taskbar (bar at the bottom of your screen) in the desktop view. You can also uninstall the program from here by clicking on "Uninstall".

Moving Tiles

The tiles on your start screen can be moved around. You may have a tile at the far right side which you want to move to the left so it is always in view. To do this, position your cursor onto a tile, and keeping the left side of your mouse held down drag the tile to the required position on the screen and then release the mouse button.

Deleting tiles from Start Screen

Most new computers will have programs (tiles) on the Start Screen that you do not want so it is a good idea to remove these from this screen. To remove a program from your start screen you should right click on the relevant tile and you will see the following menu.

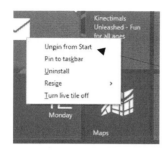

Click on Unpin from Start

You haven't deleted the program, you have merely taken it off your start screen. You may decide that you don't want the program at all, in which case another option on the menu is "uninstall program". By clicking on this, the program will be uninstalled from your computer.

Live Tiles

If you have created a Microsoft account on your computer, then some of the tiles on your start screen will be live tiles which basically means that the tiles are updating themselves all the time. One common live tile is a news program which gives you up to date headlines constantly. There are many other live tiles you can have on your start screen. You can, however, turn off these live tiles. This doesn't mean you will be removing them, you are simply turning off the constant updating of information. If you don't want the distraction of the live tiles, right click on the relevant tile and the following menu will appear.

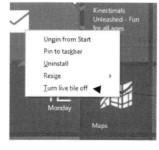

Click on "Turn live tile off", and the program will no longer update itself.

35

A More familiar view of Windows

If you have used a computer before and are used to the layout and cannot get used to Windows 8.1 and want a more familiar view of Windows then I would suggest you simply click on the Desktop tile on your start screen and you will be taken to a screen very similar to the desktop view in previous versions of Windows. You can add programs to your desktop by right clicking on a tile on the start screen and then, on the menu which has now appeared, click on Pin to taskbar.

This program will then be pinned to the bar at the bottom of your screen which is called the taskbar.

You will see on this bar the windows symbol which is your start button and by pressing on this you will be returned to the start screen where all your tiles are located.

CHAPTER ELEVEN

WINDOWS 8 HOT CORNERS

On the Start Screen the corners of the screen are very important as it is on the corners where various commands are carried out.   Just use your mouse to hover over the relevant corner as follows:

<u>Lower left corner and right clicking</u>
You will be presented with a shortcut menu (Programs and Features, Power Options, Device Manager, Task Manager etc.) You can also shut down your computer from here. In the menu which has appeared at the bottom you will see <u>shut down or sign out.</u> If you click on shut down, the computer will turn itself off.

<u>Upper left corner</u>
Shows any open windows. If you put your cursor on the top square and then, keeping it tight to the left side, move it down, all the open windows will be shown and you can now click here to switch between windows. You can also close a program from here by right clicking on it and then clicking on close.

<u>Lower right corner</u>
Shows Windows 8 Charms Bar

<u>Upper Right corner</u>
Shows Windows 8 Charms Bar

CHAPTER TWELVE

WINDOWS 8 CHARMS BAR

This bar is accessed from any program or application you are working in. There are two ways to access this bar. Firstly by hovering your mouse in the top or bottom right corners of the screen. Alternatively you can press the Windows key and C on your keyboard and by doing this you will see a box on the left which displays the current date and time, the battery status and signal strength.

On the right of the screen you will see a long vertical bar completely covering the right hand side of the screen. This is the Charms Bar. There are five buttons on this bar which are as follows starting at the top.

Search

When you click on this the following menu will appear.

From here you can type any program or app you are searching for in the small white box which has appeared on the right of the window and the results will be shown on the left of the page. Just click on the result required and you will be taken to the program.

Share

This button is used to share information with people via email or social networking sites. For instance if you have taken a screenshot of the page you are looking at, you can then click on the share button and you will have the option to email the screenshot.

Start

By pressing on this button you will be taken back to the Start Screen. An easier way to get back to the Start Screen is to press the windows key on your keyboard or clicking on the windows key at the start of your taskbar.

Devices

When you click on this button you will see the following menu appear.

Play applies if you are playing a windows game on your computer.

Print allows you to print from some apps.

The project button allows you to project your screen onto a second screen and gives you a few options to choose from.

Settings

The top half of the settings menu will be different depending on whether you are on the start screen or the desktop screen.

If you are on your start screen when you go into Settings, you will see the menu on the left. From here you can click on personalize and you will be able to change your background colour – see following pic.

Just click on the background image at the top and the colour you require and you can customize your start screen. This is the screen behind your tiles.

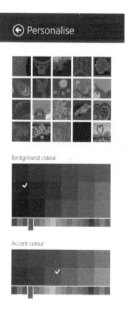

The next item on the menu is Tiles. By clicking on this you can clear all your personal information from the tiles on your start screen, particularly useful if you share your computer with other people.

The following is a screenshot of my desktop before I have cleared all personal information.

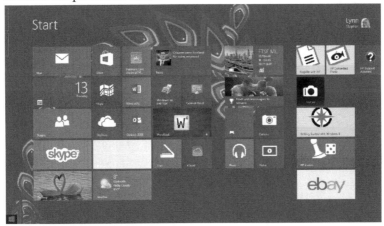

The following screenshot is after I have cleared personal information from my tiles.

You will see all the live tiles have reset themselves and no personal information is shown.

The next item in the menu is Help. If you click on this you will be taken to an internet help page.

If you are on your desktop when you click on settings, you will see the following menu.

From this menu you can access your control panel.

The personalisation on this menu will allow you to change your background picture on your desktop and set a screensaver (very similar to previous versions of windows).

By clicking on PC Info you will be taken to a screen setting out all the information about your computer, for instance it will show the version of windows you are using, the processor installed in your computer together with the memory installed.

By clicking on Help, this will take you to a Help and Support page. Click in the search box at the top and type your question, press enter on your keyboard and the solution to your question should appear.

CHAPTER THIRTEEN

TURNING OFF YOUR COMPUTER

There are several ways to turn off your computer. Firstly you need to bring up your charms bar. You can do this by putting your cursor in either the top or bottom right hand corners or pressing the windows key and c on your keyboard. Both of these actions will bring up the charms bar. From here you should click on the cog (settings), then click on power and then click on shutdown. Your computer will now shut down.

Another way to shut down your computer is to right click on the bottom left corner and on the menu which has now appeared hover your cursor over Shut down or sign out and then move over to the next small menu and click on Shut down. Your computer will now shut down.

You should always turn your computer off in this way and never by using the power button on the computer itself.

CHAPTER FOURTEEN

USING THE INTERNET

Internet Explorer Explained

On the Start Screen you will see a tile called Internet Explorer. This is the program used to explore the internet and is known as a browser. Internet Explorer will enable you to visit websites and find out information. There are websites about all sorts of subjects and most organisations have one. There is virtually nothing you cannot find out on the internet. You can search for information, book holidays, online shopping, use social networking sites, watch BBC iPlayer etc. – the list is endless.

You will have to use your mouse to move around the internet pages. You simply move your mouse and this controls the pointer on the screen. You will have to click the left side of the mouse to issue an instruction or choose an option. This is usually an arrow but will change to the following symbol $\underline{\text{I}}$ when you point it to a space where you wish to type text. When your cursor changes to a hand, this means that you can click here and you will be taken to a new page.

On a Windows 8.1 computer there are two ways in which you can access the internet. One way is by clicking on the Internet Explorer tile on your start screen. This version of Internet Explorer is primarily for tablets and mobile phones and I think for the more advanced user. I personally prefer the desktop version of Internet Explorer as it has all the relevant toolbars and is much easier to use. Therefore as a beginner I would suggest you click on your "Desktop" tile on your start screen. At the bottom of the page on the bar you will see the Internet Explorer icon (blue e). Click once on this and you will be taken to the internet home page which has been set on your computer. See following picture.

You will see that I have my internet home page set to Google as I find this very easy to use and is ideal if you are a beginner. In the centre of the screen you will see a long white box (under the word Google) and it is in this box that you should type whatever you are looking for. You need to first click in this box until you see a flashing cursor – you are now able to type in this box.

Bear in mind that the more information you put in the search box the better the results will be. Once you have typed what you are looking for into the box, press enter on your keyboard and you will then see a long list of websites which will be relevant to your search.   As you start to type the subject you are searching for, Google will predict what you are looking for and give you alternatives at the top of the page.   The results of the search are shown in a list as per the following picture.   In this instance I have searched for "computing for beginners" and a list of relevant websites has appeared relating to this subject.

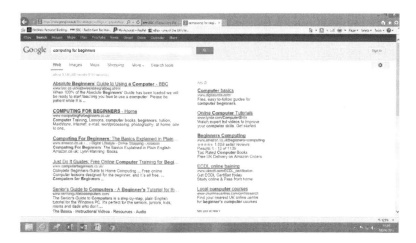

When you search for something you always get a long list of results, sometimes thousands but I always find it is the top 15-20 which are the most relevant. To select one of the results, you should click on the one you wish to look at (make sure your cursor is a hand before you click) and you will be taken to the website of your choice.   My website is the second in the list so to go to this website you would click on "COMPUTING FOR BEGINNERS".

When you have clicked on the website you wish to view from the list, the first page you will see will be the homepage of that particular site.

Every website will have a homepage which will show various links to different parts of that website. The following is a picture of my home page.

From this you will see that I have seven links at the top of the page which are Home, Computer Training, iPad training, Book 1 – The Basics, Book 2 – Next Step, Book 3 – Windows 8 and Contact Information. By clicking on any of these you will be taken to the relevant section of the website.

If you move your cursor, which at the moment is an arrow, over a heading you will notice that the cursor has now changed to a hand and it is now you should click to be taken to this particular page of the website.

If you now go back to the top and click on "Home" you will be taken back to the first page of the website. It is basically like turning the pages in a book. As long as the cursor is a hand when you click you will be taken to a different page of the website.

When you have finished looking at a particular website and wish to view another, you should click on the house symbol on the bar at the top of the page. This will automatically take you back to the home page which has been set on your computer. In my case, it takes me back to Google.

Favourites

If you think you will be looking at the same website many times then it is a good idea to put it in your favourites list or on your favourites bar at the top of the page. To add a website to your favourites list you must first be on the website, then click on the star symbol (next to the house symbol) and the following window will appear.

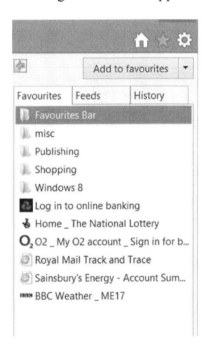

At the top of this window you will see "Add to Favourites". You should click once on this and the following small box appears in the centre of the screen:

Just click on "Add" and this website will then be added to your favourites list.

To access this website next time you use the internet, just click on the star at the top of the page and a list of your favourites will appear, click once on the website required and you will be taken straight to that website.

To add a website to your favourites bar is very simple. When you are on the website you wish to add, just click once on the yellow star with the green arrow on it on the top left (see picture below) and the website will be added to your favourites bar and will always be visible when you first open the Internet.

You will see I have my Banking page on my favourites bar. To access anything on your favourites bar you simply click once on the website name and you will be taken straight to that website.

Back/Forward Buttons

To move back or forward a page on Internet Explorer you will see two arrows at the top left of your screen. To move back a page click on the left button and to move forward a page click on the right button. You can also use the Backspace key on your keyboard to go back a page.

<u>Staying Safe on the Internet</u>

When and if you decide to buy things from the internet there are two main things you must look out for. Firstly when you are asked to enter personal information and credit card details, there should be a padlock symbol in the address bar at the top of the page *(see following picture)*.

Also at the beginning of the website address the *http* should now read *https*. The *s* stands for secure.
If the paddock or the https is not there **DO NOT** continue as this site will not be secure.

CHAPTER FIFTEEN

EMAILS

E-Mail (short for electronic mail) is a quick and easy way to keep in touch with people. Your messages are sent and received instantly. You can send messages to people on the other side of the world and they will be received instantly.

Live Mail

In order to use the email program in Windows 8.1, Live Mail, you need to create a Microsoft Account. You may have done this when you set up your Computer. Live Mail is accessed by clicking the Mail tile on your start screen. You can set up a number of email accounts in here.

Reading your Emails

When you click on the Mail tile on your start screen a window similar to the one below will appear.

The window will be very similar to the one above if you have received an email. This window will have three symbols at the top right.

However, if you have no emails the window will look like the following and there will only be one symbol at the top right.

I will explain the symbols further on in this chapter.

This window is split into three sections, the first section which is dark blue shows your email folders which are as follows:

Inbox (Envelope):	This is where all new emails will be placed.
Drafts:	Unfinished emails are stored in here for you to finish later.
Sent Mail:	A copy of all messages you have sent are stored in this folder.
Outbox:	Emails temporarily go in here prior to being sent.
Junk:	This is where the junk emails will be put. Junk mail is very similar to junk mail you receive in the post and which is not needed. You should always check this folder because sometimes messages are put in here which are NOT junk.
Deleted/Trash	There is where all the emails you delete, from whichever folder, will be stored and this folder should be emptied from time to time.

The second section of this window is where all your emails will appear. To read an email click on the email in the second column and the text of the email will be shown in the third column.

Symbols

The first of these symbols will enable you to reply or forward the email message you have received. The second symbol, when clicked on, will bring up a new email window, and the third symbol will delete the email and place it in your Deleted/Trash folder.

Sending an Email

To send an email you must first click on the + symbol at the top right of the page.

This will bring up the following window:

On the right of the page you will see To: In the box to the right of this, type in the email address of the person you are sending the message to. Be very careful when entering email addresses as a small mistake will result in the email not being sent.

Once you have done this you should click on the words "Add a Subject". Here you will type the subject of your message i.e. if your email is about a holiday your subject would be "holiday".

You should then click on the words "add a message" and type your message. Your message can be as short or long as you want. Once you have finished typing your message, you should click on the first symbol at the top right of the page.

Your email will now be sent and will be received in a matter of minutes, wherever in the world it has been sent. It's as easy as that.

You can see copies of all emails you have sent by clicking on the Sent Mail folder on the left of the page which will show the date and time the message was sent.

Replying to an Email

If you have received an email which you wish to reply to you should click on the first symbol at the top right of the page. You will then see a small menu appear which has three options Reply, Reply All and Forward. You should click on reply and you can then type your reply where the cursor is flashing. When you have finished click on the first symbol at the top of the screen which will send your email.

Forwarding an Email

If you have received an email which you wish to forward to another person you should click on the first symbol at the top right of the page and on the menu which appears, click on forward and then enter the email address of the person you wish to forward the message to. Click on the send symbol (the first symbol at the right of the page) and your message will be forwarded.

Deleting Emails

Once you have read your messages and no longer wish to keep them, click once on the dustbin symbol at the top right of the window and this will place it into your Deleted/Trash folder. It will not be permanently deleted until you clear your Deleted/Trash folder.

Clearing Deleted/Trash Folder

Once you are sure that all the messages which have been placed in your Deleted/Trash folder are no longer required, you should empty this folder. To do this, click on Deleted/Trash in your folder list.

You will see all the emails which you have deleted in here. Right at the top above the first email you will see the word All. If you more your cursor to this word a small box will appear to the left of the word All. Click in this box and a tick will appear which is selecting all the emails at once. You can now click on the dustbin symbol on the right of the page and all the messages will be deleted.

Remember when you have emptied this folder, you cannot get the messages back so be absolutely certain before doing this.

Sending Attachments

You may wish to send an attachment with your email i.e. a photo or document. To do this, after you have bought up a new message window, you should click on the paperclip symbol at the top right of the page.

A window similar to the following will appear. This will normally open up showing your pictures folders.

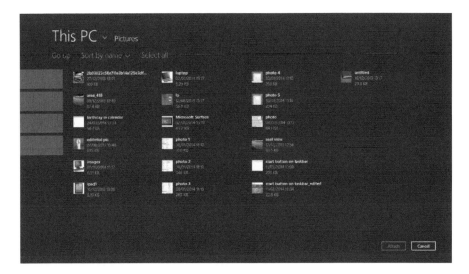

From here you just click on the picture you wish to attach, or if you wish to send more than one, click on each one in turn and then click on attach at the bottom right of the screen and your pictures will be attached to your email.

If you wish to send a document as an attachment then on the window which appears after you click on the paperclip symbol, you will need to click on Go up – see following.

You will then see a screen similar to the following:

From here you should click on Documents and all your document files will appear. Click on the document to send, then on attach at the bottom right and your document will be attached to your email.

Type your message and then click on send and your message and your attachment will be sent.

Opening an Attachment

If you receive an email which has an attachment with it, you will see one of the following beneath the email.

If you have received a picture then it will be the box on the left which you will see. Alternatively if you have been sent a document then you will see the box in the middle. If it is a PDF attachment, it will be similar to the box on the right.

If you just click once on the relevant box the attachment will open and you will be able to view it.

If you wish to save the attachment to your computer then you should right click on the relevant box and a menu will appear giving you the option to Open With or Save.

Click on save and you will see a screen similar to the following.

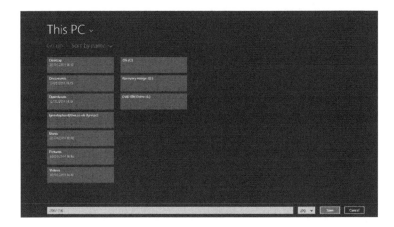

You should click on the place where you wish to save the attachment i.e. if it is a picture you should save it into Pictures and if it is a text or pdf file you should save it into Documents. Once you have selected the folder to save the attachment into, you should click on "Save" at the bottom of the page. Your attachment is now saved into your folder and the email can be deleted.

Printing an Email

If you have received an email which you wish to print you should right click on the email and the following bar will appear at the bottom of the screen. Click on more at the end and then click on print.

You will then see on the right of the screen a Print menu has appeared. See following picture.

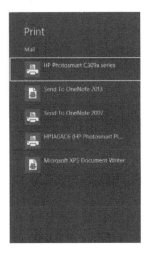

The menu which has appeared shows the different printer options available. You should locate your printer name and click once on it and the following window will appear.

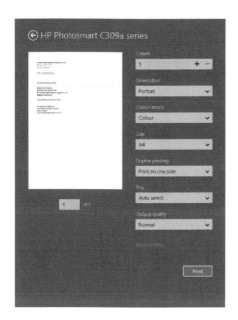

You will see that the menu on the right of the window allows you to select the amount of copies you require, the paper size etc. If you just want to print one copy, these settings can stay the same and you simply click on the Print button at the bottom right of the screen. The email will now be printed.

CHAPTER SIXTEEN

CONTACTS

Adding Contacts

In Windows 8.1 adding contacts into an address book is done by clicking on the People Tile on your Start Screen.

When you click on this tile, a window similar to the following will appear.

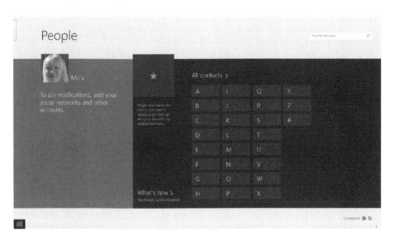

If you now right click anywhere on the screen you will see a bar at the bottom of the screen and on the right hand side of this bar you should click on New contact.

The following window will now appear.

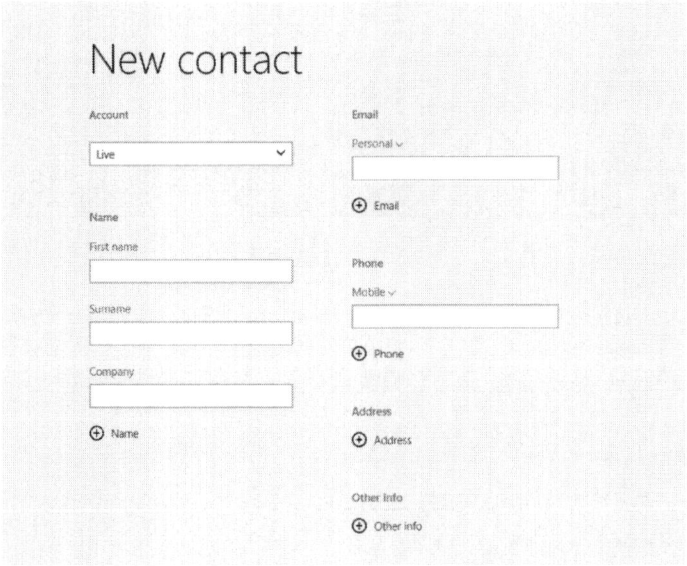

New contact

Account

Live

Name

First name

Surname

Company

⊕ Name

Email

Personal ⌄

⊕ Email

Phone

Mobile ⌄

⊕ Phone

Address

⊕ Address

Other Info

⊕ Other info

You now need to fill in the various boxes on this page. You must first click in the relevant box until a flashing cursor appears indicating that you can now type in this box. When all boxes have been completed you will see two symbols at the top right of the screen.   You should click on the first symbol which is save.

Your contact has now been added and a window similar to the following will appear.

If you now click on the arrow to the left of your contact's name you will be taken back to the first screen and you can now begin again by right clicking and clicking on new contact etc.

Amending/Deleting Contact details

If one of your contacts changes their email address then you can easily amend their details by again clicking on the People tile and then click on All Contacts. You will now see all your contacts. Click on the contact to amend and then right click and you will see a bar has appeared at the bottom of the window (*see following picture*).

If you now click on the Edit symbol you will be able to go into the contact's details and amend any information. You can also delete a contact by following the above steps but instead of clicking on edit, click on Delete. Once you have finished, remember to click on the Save symbol at the top to save any changes you have made.

CHAPTER SEVENTEEN

PHOTOS

On your start screen, you will see a tile named Photos. This is where you find all the photos you have transferred to your computer from your camera.

Transferring photos from your camera

When you connect a camera to your computer via a USB lead, a window similar to the following will appear.

Obviously this may differ depending on which make of camera you are using. On this menu you should click on

Import photos and videos and a window similar to the following will appear.

On this window you will see all the photos in your camera have been selected (indicated by ticks). You should now click on import at the bottom right of the screen.

Your photos have now been imported to your computer.

Viewing your Photos

In order to view your photos, you should click on the Photos tile and the relevant folder will be identified by the date on which the photos were transferred to your computer.

Click on this folder and you will see your photos inside. Click on a picture and it will bring it up larger. If you wish to view a slideshow of your photos you should right click anywhere on your screen and you will see a bar appear at the bottom. Click on slideshow.

Rename a Folder

It is a good idea when you have transferred your photos to rename the folder to something which you will easily recognise.

To do this you should right click on the folder to rename which will place a tick in the top right corner and will also bring up a bar at the bottom of the screen – see following.

On the left hand side of this bar you will see four symbols. You need to click on Rename and you will see the following:

Type the new name into the box and then click on rename.

Deleting unwanted photos

To delete any photos from your computer you should right click on each photo to delete which will place a tick in the top right of that photo and then click on Delete on the bar which has appeared at the bottom of the screen.

Printing your Photos

To print a photo you should click on your Photos tile on the start screen then click on the folder containing the photo you wish to print. Click once on the photo to print and then hold down the Ctrl key and at the same time press the P on your keyboard and you will see a window similar to the following.

On the right of this window you will see a list of printing options. From this list you should click on your printer and the following will appear.

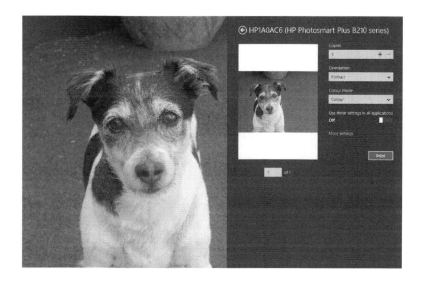

On the right of this window you can select how many copies you require, whether you want your photo to be portrait or landscape and whether you wish to print in colour or black and white. Further down on this menu you will see 'More Settings'. If you click on this you will see a window similar to the following.

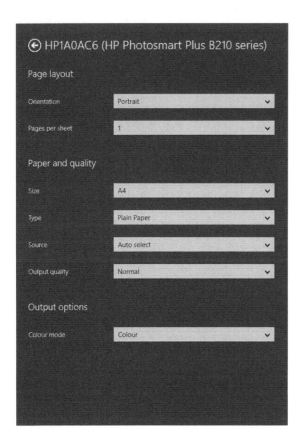

From here you can select the size of paper you are using, the type of paper, i.e. plain paper or glossy photo paper and choose the output quality of your print. For instance if you select to put this on high quality you will get the best possible print of your photo. Alternatively you could put it on draft quality and you will get a print which will use considerably less ink.

When you have made your selections you should click on the back arrow at the top of the page which will return you to the previous page where you can now select Print. Your photo will now be printed.

CHAPTER EIGHTEEN

FILES AND FOLDERS

All your files and folders are kept in Libraries on your computer. To find these you should click on "File Explorer" which is a tile on your Start Screen (if this tile is not on your start screen you can pin it to the Start Screen). You can also locate this folder by clicking on your desktop tile. File Explorer is the second icon shown on the taskbar at the bottom of the screen. See following.

When you click on File Explorer, the following window will appear. You will see four items shown in the main part of this window, Documents, Music, Pictures and Videos.

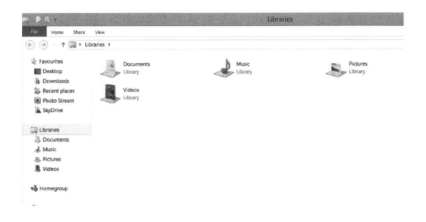

As a beginner you will probably only be using the Documents and Pictures folders. Briefly all music and videos which you transfer to your computer will be placed into the relevant folder.

When you create a piece of work (letters etc.) which you wish to keep, these are called files and are saved in your Documents folder. You can have as many files in your Documents folder as you like but it is always a good idea to keep things tidy.

Although your Documents folder is the main folder where all your files will be kept, you can make separate folders in this main folder to store your work so it is easily found. For example you could make a folder called "Personal Letters" into which all the letters you write will be stored and another folder called "Business Letters" into which all the business letters will be stored.

This makes it easy for you to find your saved files. You can have as many folders as you like in your Documents folder.

The same applies to your Pictures folder, each photo you transfer is called a file and you can make folders in your

Pictures folder to easily identify your photos. For example you could make a folder called "Holiday 2014" and store all your holiday photos in here. Again you can have as many folders as you like.

Making a New Folder

If you double click on documents or pictures and then click on the home tab at the top of the screen the following toolbar will appear.

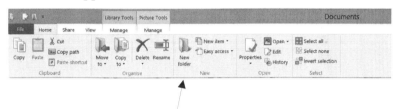

You can now make a new folder by clicking on "New Folder". You will now see the following folder on the screen.

Just type in the name for your folder (no need to click as the text is highlighted and whatever you type will replace this). Press enter on your keyboard and your new folder is made.

Moving a file into a Folder (drag and drop)

Once you have made your new folder you can move your file into this folder. The easiest way to do this is to drag and drop the file into the folder. To do this you need to place your cursor over the file to be moved, hold down the left side of your mouse, and keeping it held down, drag the file over the top of the folder into which your file is to be moved. Now let go of the left side of the mouse and your file will have disappeared from your screen, as it is now inside the folder. To check it is there you can double click on the folder and you will see your file.

To open your file from within the folder, simply double click on it and it will open in the program which created it.

Renaming a File or Folder

There are two ways to rename a file or folder. Firstly you should click once on the file or folder to rename, so it is highlighted then either:

a) On the home tab click on Rename, type the new name for your file or folder, press enter on your keyboard and the file or folder is renamed.

b) Right click on the file or folder to rename, click on Rename, type the new name for your file or folder, and press enter on your keyboard and the file or folder is renamed.

Deleting a File or Folder

There are three ways you can delete a file or folder. Firstly you should click on the file or folder to be deleted, so it is highlighted, then either:

a) On the home tab click on Delete.

b) Right click on the file or folder and then click on Delete.

82

c) Press Delete on your keyboard.

Creating a file in Documents

When you are in your word-processing program and have typed a document which you wish to save, e.g. a letter, you should click on the File tab at the top left of your word-processing screen. See toolbar below.

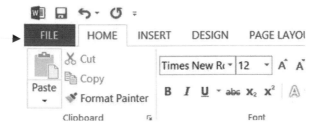

When you click on File the following menu will appear.

You should now click on "Save As" and a Window similar to the following will appear.

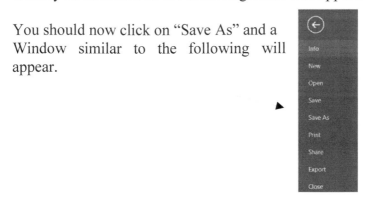

In the second column click on "Computer" and in the third column click on "My Documents". A window similar to the following will now appear.

83

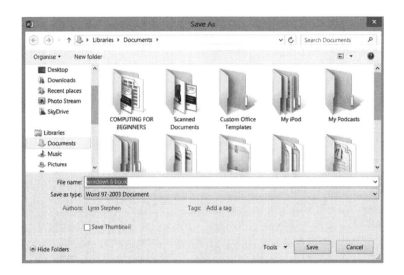

Where you see the highlighted text in the File name box, you should type the name of your document. There is no need to click in this box, as when text is highlighted, as soon as you start to type, this will replace the highlighted text.

You should then click on Save at the bottom right of this window and your document will have been saved into your Documents folder.

If you have chosen to set your computer to back up your files automatically to OneDrive (see Backing Up chapter) then your files will automatically be saved to OneDrive and you just need to name the file and click on Save, as above.

Pictures Folder

When you transfer your photos from your camera to your computer (as shown in Photos section) your pictures will not only be found in the Windows 8.1 Photos app but will also be in your Pictures folder in Windows Explorer.

From your pictures folder, you can also view and print your pictures.

Finding your Saved Work

When you want to view your saved documents or pictures you should click on the file explorer icon after which your Libraries window will appear:

If your files are saved to your computer then you should double click on Documents in the main window and all your files and folders in the main Documents folder will be shown. Double click on the item to view and the file will open in the program in which it was created i.e. a letter will open in your word-processing program.

The same applies to view a photo. Double click on the Pictures folder, then double click on the folder containing the picture you wish to view and then double click on the picture to view it in a larger format.

If you have chosen to save your work to OneDrive you should click on this in the menu on the left hand side and then follow the same steps as before.

▶

CHAPTER NINETEEN

BACKING UP

The most important thing you should do regularly is back up your work, whether it be pictures or documents as if your computer were to go wrong, there is a strong possibility that all your documents and pictures will be lost.   Similarly if you have a virus on your computer, you could lose all your files.

OneDrive (formerly SkyDrive)

If you have a Microsoft account on your computer you can back up your documents and pictures to an online storage facility called OneDrive.   Microsoft give you 7 GB of free storage and you can buy more at any time.

There are advantages to backing up to an online storage program.   If your computer were to go wrong and you hadn't backed up your work, it is highly likely that you will lose all your photos and documents which are of course irreplaceable.

With OneDrive you can set your computer to save all your items to this drive and not to your computer. The files are still accessible from your computer but are not actually stored on the computer. Therefore if something were to happen to your computer, all your files are safe on OneDrive.

Another advantage to online storage is that you can access it from any computer. For instance say you had a desktop computer and also a laptop, you can save your work to OneDrive and then access it from either computer.

Setting Up OneDrive

To set your computer to automatically back up to OneDrive you should go to Settings by going to the bottom right of your screen (same as turning off). Click on the cog and at the bottom of the window which has now appeared (see following picture) click on Change PC Settings.

On the window which has now appeared click on OneDrive.

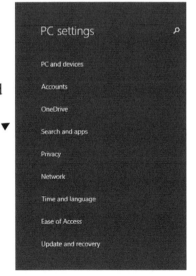

On the next window which appears click on File Storage and then on the right hand side click on the small box underneath the words "save documents to OneDrive by default" it should now say On – see following picture.

Your files will now automatically be backed up to OneDrive and can be accessed from any computer.

Press your windows key on your keyboard to return to your start screen

Memory Sticks

The most reliable way to manually back up your work is to use a memory stick. There are various sorts of memory stick but most will be similar to those shown in the following picture.

Memory sticks come in various sizes i.e. 1GB, 2GB, 4GB, 8GB, 16GB, 32GB and 64GB are the most popular sizes. You should choose the size which will represent the amount of data you have to back up. For instance if you have hundreds of photos to back up, I would go for one with a larger capacity like the 16GB or 32GB. If you only have a few documents to back up then a 2GB or 4GB stick would be sufficient. Again it all depends on how much data you have to back up or may in future have to back up as you can add more files to your memory stick as and when needed.

Once you have your memory stick, you should insert this into a USB slot on your computer and a window similar to the following will appear.

You will see on the bar at the top of this window the name of your memory stick. I am using a Kingston memory stick. You will also see in the list on the left hand side that the Kingston memory stick has appeared under the Computer heading.

If you now click on Documents, or whatever folder you wish to back up from, in the left hand menu, a window similar to the following will appear.

To copy (back up) a file or folder onto the memory stick you should position your cursor over the file or folder to be moved, hold down the left side of the mouse and then drag it over to the memory stick (i.e. Kingston). When you have your file or folder positioned over the memory stick it will say "Copy to Kingston" (*see following picture*). At this point you should release the mouse button and the file or folder will have been placed onto the memory stick.

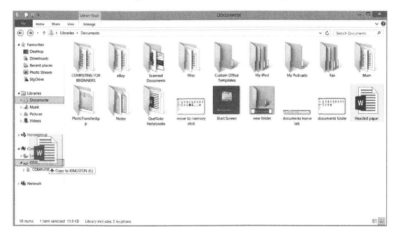

You can now remove the memory stick from the computer and keep it safe knowing that should anything happen to your computer, your files are backed up.

Adding to your Memory Stick

You can add more documents to your memory stick at any time by following the steps above.

Viewing items on your Memory Stick

To see at any time what documents or pictures are stored on your memory stick, simply insert it into a USB slot on your computer and a window will appear showing exactly what files are saved onto your memory stick.

Deleting items from your Memory Stick

If you wish to delete any items from your memory stick, this can easily be done. When you insert the memory stick into a usb slot on your computer, a window will appear showing all items on the memory stick.

To delete an item, right click on it and then click on delete, on the menu which has now appeared, and the item will now be removed from the memory stick.

ABOUT THE AUTHOR

Lynn Stephen recovered from a ten year battle with ME in 1999 and re-trained in computers. She went on to obtain various City & Guild qualifications and in 2002, set up her computer training business "Computing for Beginners" which gives one to one training to the beginner. This is now a successful business and keeps Lynn very busy.

Lynn has previously written three books "Computing for Beginners – The Basics Explained in Plain English" which covers the absolute basics of computing and "Computing for Beginners – The Next Step" which goes a step further into digital photograph, word-processing, and more. In 2013 Lynn wrote her first Windows 8 book, "Windows 8 Explained in Plain English" but due to the many updates which Microsoft have applied, she has felt the need to update her book to cover Windows 8.1.

Once again this book is aimed at the complete beginner. However, she is confident that this book will also benefit those who are already computer literate but who are not familiar with Windows 8.1.

Other titles available by Lynn Stephen

Computing for Beginners – The Basics Explained in Plain English
Computing for Beginners – The Next Step
Computing for Beginners – Windows 8 Explained in Plain English

Printed in Great Britain
by Amazon.co.uk, Ltd.,
Marston Gate.